THE CONSUMER IMPACT OF REPEAL OF 14(b)

Marshall R. Colberg

With a Foreword by

Sam J. Ervin

U.S. Senator, North Carolina
1954-75

The Heritage Foundation

Washington, D.C.

MARSHALL R. COLBERG is Professor of Economics (and former chairman of the department) at Florida State University. He received his B.A. and M.A. degrees from the University of Chicago and his Ph.D. from the University of Michigan. Before coming to Florida State University he was an economist with various government agencies, including the Civilian Production Administration and the U.S. Air Force. He is a former president of the Southern Economic Association and is a member of the Mont Pelerin Society. He is the author of *Human Capital in Southern Development: 1939–1963* and the co-author of *Prices, Income and Public Policy*, of *Business Economics* and of *Factors in the Location of Florida Industry*. He has published numerous economic studies in the *Journal of Political Economy*, the *Southern Economic Journal*, the *Journal of Finance*, the *National Tax Journal* and other professional journals.

SAM. J. ERVIN, the author of the Foreword, represented North Carolina in the United States Senate from 1954 to 1975. Before his election to the Senate he served as an Associate Justice of the Supreme Court of North Carolina. In the Senate he served as Chairman of the Subcommittee on Constitutional Rights of the Judiciary Committee.

Library of Congress Cataloging in Publication Data

77-17061

ISBN 0-89195-021-4

513 C Street, NE
Washington, DC 20002

Foreword

It was not all that long ago—in 1965 and 1966—that the last major effort was made to repeal Section 14(b) of the Taft-Hartley Act, and destroy Right-to-Work laws. I was proud at the time to play a major role in the defense of these laws.

Professor Colberg, of course, has quite a different perspective on Right-to-Work laws. His is the eye of a trained economist. Mine is that of a country lawyer, who would rather spend his days fishing.

While his objection to destroying Right-to-Work laws has as its foundation a studiously arrived-at conclusion that universal compulsory unionism would disrupt the national economy—and fuel inflation and unemployment—mine is based on a sixty-year career as a student and partisan of the United States Constitution and all that it stands for.

It does not take a man of great learning, really, to know that the cornerstone of our society is freedom. Likewise, it does not take a philosopher to understand that compulsory unionism—forcing people to join or pay money to unwanted labor unions—violates individual freedom.

Through the ages, the right to work and sustain one's self and one's family has been recognized not only as one of mankind's most basic freedoms—but as an obligation as well. Those who would deny the right to work to citizens of this country, simply because of their membership or non-membership in labor organizations, are asking us to turn our backs on more than 200 years of Constitutional law and the centuries of religious and social traditions that link us with past generations.

Though I urge all thoughtful Americans to read Professor Colberg's report, it is not without a sense of shame. Not shame in what he says, but in the fact that the right to work should even be subject to debate.

Because in the final analysis, what we're talking about here is freedom. There should be no need for me or anyone else to defend this freedom.

SAM J. ERVIN
U.S. Senate
1954–75

1

Enactment of Section 14(b) and Development of State Right-to-Work Laws

14(b) Nothing in this Act shall be construed as authorizing the execution or application of agreements requiring membership in a labor organization as a condition of employment in any state or territory in which such execution or application is prohibited by state or territorial law.[1]

The Taft-Hartley Act amendments to the National Labor Relations Act, passed in 1947 over Presidential veto, reflect an uneasy Congressional compromise between a belief that Federal law should promote and favor union growth and a belief that competition and individual choice should prevail in the labor market. The Taft-Hartley Act outlaws the closed shop[2] outright but permits the union shop[3] except where the individual states, as authorized by the famous Section 14(b), pass Right-to-Work laws. These state laws, which may also be called "Voluntary Unionism" laws, permit workers to join unions only if they wish to do so, even where collective bargaining takes place involving a unit in which they work.

State Right-to-Work Laws

Even before passage of the Taft-Hartley Act in 1947, several states incorporated Right-to-Work provisions in their constitutions. Florida and Arkansas led the way in 1944; Arizona and South Dakota followed in November 1946, and Nebraska in December of that year.

---

[1] 29 U.S. Code 164(b).

[2] Requires that a job-seeker be a member of the union in order to be eligible for hiring and must maintain that membership in order to retain his job.

[3] The worker need not be a member of the union at the time of hiring but must join within a specified period—usually 30 days—to retain his job; he must also retain that membership or lose his job.

Other early Right-to-Work states (1947 and 1948) were Georgia, North Carolina, Tennessee, Virginia, Texas, and North Dakota, all adopting Right-to-Work provisions chiefly by statute. About ten years later a flurry of state legislation brought the number of Right-to-Work states to nineteen. The composition of the group changed slightly when Wyoming was added in February 1963 and Indiana dropped out in February 1965. The number of Right-to-Work states was increased to the present number—twenty—in July 1976 when the Louisiana legislature passed such a law. The twenty states (and the Territory of American Samoa) with either a Right-to-Work statute, constitutional amendment, or both, are Alabama, Arizona, Arkansas, Florida, Georgia, Iowa, Kansas, Louisiana, Mississippi, Nebraska, Nevada, North Carolina, North Dakota, South Carolina, South Dakota, Tennessee, Texas, Utah, Virginia and Wyoming.

Although most of the state Right-to-Work laws either fail to provide penalties for violations or provide only that violations are misdemeanors, the majority of statutes permit suits against violators and/or provide for injunctive relief from violations.[4] Consequently, the direct effects of these laws are embodied in a vast number of court decisions and actions spanning a period of over thirty years.

Florida passed the first Right-to-Work law in 1944 in the form of a constitutional amendment which provided the following:

> The right of persons to work shall not be denied or abridged on account of membership or non-membership in any labor union or labor organization; provided, that this clause shall not be construed to deny or abridge the right of employees by and through a labor organization or labor union to bargain collectively with their employer.

There is a striking similarity between this wording and that of all the subsequent constitutional amendments and statutes on the subject.[5] North Carolina has the most detailed law, part of which is quoted below; it is an especially complete and clear statute:

> The General Assembly of North Carolina do enact:
>
> Section 1. The right to live includes the right to work. The exercise of the right to work must be protected and maintained free from undue restraints and coercion. It is hereby declared to be the public policy of North Carolina that the right of persons to work shall not be denied or abridged on account of membership or non-membership in any labor union or labor organization or association.

[4] Paul Sultan, *Right-to-Work Laws: A Study in Conflict* (Los Angeles: Institute of Industrial Relations, University of California, 1958), pp. 60–61.

[5] J. R. Dempsey, *The Operation of the Right-to-Work Laws* (Milwaukee: Marquette University Press, 1961), p. 2.

Section 2. Any agreement or combination between any employer and any labor union or labor organization whereby persons not members of such union or organization shall be denied the right to work for said employer, or whereby such membership is made a condition of employment or continuation of employment by such employer, or whereby any such union or organization acquires an employment monopoly in any enterprise, is hereby declared to be against the public policy and an illegal combination or conspiracy in restraint of trade or commerce in the State of North Carolina.

Section 3. No person shall be required by an employer to become or to remain a member of any labor union or labor organization as a condition of employment or continuation of employment by such employer.

Section 4. No person shall be required by an employer to abstain or refrain from membership in any labor union or labor organization as a condition of employment or continuation of employment.

Section 5. No employer shall require any person, as a condition of employment or continuation of employment, to pay any dues, fees, or other charges of any kind to any labor union or labor organization.

The Agency Shop

The "agency shop" agreement results in evasion of state Right-to-Work laws. This clause in collective bargaining agreements does not require compulsory union membership but does require instead that non-union persons pay the union a fee equivalent to union dues in order to be allowed to retain their jobs. Some state Right-to-Work laws specifically outlaw agency shop situations (as in Section 5 of the North Carolina law) as well as the union shop.

Unions argue that they are required to bargain collectively for all persons within the bargaining unit—union members and non-members alike. They contend that under these circumstances it is only fair that they be able to collect from everyone in the unit, thus preventing non-union workers from receiving benefits of collective bargaining without paying their share of bargaining costs. However, non-joiners are likely to feel that they are not helped but actually hurt by the activity of the union. It is notable that unions have insisted on the right to bargain for entire working groups, including both union and non-union members, and are unwilling to seek a change in this aspect of the law.

There is a long history of court decisions regarding the agency shop. In 1962 the Florida State Supreme Court held that the agency shop violated the constitutional amendment which constitutes that state's Right-to-Work law. The Court's opinion included the following:

> The natural and reasonable interpretation of the Florida constitutional amendment which prohibits compulsory membership in a labor organization as a condition of employment or of continued employment, is that it

necessarily forbids forcing a non-member employee to pay union initiation fees, dues and assessments or equivalent amounts as a condition of employment or continued employment. A contrary construction of the right to work law would leave it little or no useful purpose to serve.[6]

In Indiana, where the Right-to-Work law was repealed in 1965, the State Supreme Court did not hold the agency shop to be in violation of the law. However, rulings in other Right-to-Work states during the same general time period were similar to the Florida decision. The rulings pertained to Arizona (1954); Kansas (1961); Nebraska (1960); Nevada (1962); North Carolina (1962); North Dakota (1959); South Dakota (1958); and Texas (1961).[7]

An especially interesting ruling was made recently in California, which is not a Right-to-Work state and in which the union shop is consequently legal. The case involved the Brotherhood of Railway and Airline Clerks. The Court ruled against the use of agency shop dues for organizing, publishing membership newspapers, holding conventions, and paying per capita dues to the union.[8] This represents a change from an earlier California ruling which upheld the suspension of a famous Californian, Cecil B. deMille, who was put off the air by his union (AFRA) for refusing to contribute a dollar assessed by the union for a political purpose.[9]

---

[6] *Schermerhorn v. Local 1625, Retail Clerks*, 141 So. 2d 269, 276.

[7] T. J. Hailstones, B. L. Martin, G. A. Wing, *Contemporary Economic Problems and Issues* (Cincinnati: South-Western, 1966), p. 179.

[8] "Right-to-Work Gains Shake the Union Shop," *Business Week*, February 16, 1976, p. 26.

[9] E. A. Keller, *The Case for the Right-to-Work Laws*, (Chicago: The Heritage Foundation, 1956), pp. 47-48.

2

Summary of Impact

Impact on Regional Economic Development

In part, the dispute over Section 14(b) may be regarded as a question of how to preserve competition among regions in economic development. Those who favor retention of state Right-to-Work laws favor allocation of resources through the price system in our basically free market economy. Thus, states with relatively abundant labor supplies (usually these are Southern states) may be attractive on a labor-cost basis to labor-intensive industry, thereby attracting investment to these states. Repeal of Right-to-Work laws would work to reduce or eliminate wage rate competition between regions.

The need for economic development is especially critical in those states which have relatively abundant supplies of unskilled and semi-skilled labor; many of the states which have Right-to-Work laws are among such states. Currently, these states are also gaining in relative working-age population. The rate of population growth in the past six years has been roughly twice as rapid in the Right-to-Work states as in the other states, creating a need for heavy capital investment to provide employment in these regions. Economists who have studied regional economic development usually feel that the growth of labor unions in the South would lessen the region's competitive advantage in wage rates and would thereby slow down the relative rate of investment in the region. In fact, the Southward migration of whole industries, such as the textile industry, has been heavily motivated by unionism in the Northern states.

There is evidence that the Right-to-Work laws have been helpful in attracting new manufacturing, especially of the labor-intensive varieties. As is shown in Chapter Three, Table 3.6, the nineteen states that have had such laws for two or three decades have gained quite remarkably in their proportion of the nation's manufacturing employment. From about 19 percent in 1958 the proportion rose to over 25 percent in 1972. Such figures imply the converse: in the states that do not have voluntary unionism laws there is a reduction in relative employment. It is notable that Louisiana, in spite of its excellent materials base and location for transportation (see Appendix), made no gain in this respect from 1958 to 1967 and only a modest gain between 1967 and 1972. It is not surprising then that the Louisiana legislature felt a need to pass a Right-to-Work law in 1976. In spite of contrary claims by some labor economists, the Right-to-Work laws *do* seem to be important to the economic development of a state.

The importance of Right-to-Work laws, lower labor costs, and special incentives such as labor-training programs in attracting foreign investment and thereby providing domestic employment should not be overlooked. For example, South Carolina attracted $300 million in foreign capital in 1975, bringing total foreign investment in that state's manufacturing facilities to over $1.43 billion and providing employment for 19,300 of its residents. Six other Southern states have also attracted substantial foreign investment: Alabama, Florida, Georgia, Mississippi, North Carolina, and Tennessee.[10] All have Right-to-Work laws. In an era when there is often a charge that American multinational corporations with facilities abroad are exporting jobs, the importation of jobs through foreign investment in the United States is welcomed.[11] The repeal of Section 14(b) would greatly reduce the competitive attraction which Right-to-Work states currently hold over other foreign labor markets. The opponents of 14(b) and of state Right-to-Work laws believe that equity requires rapid unionization of the South and Southwest to raise costs of production toward levels that exist in the more heavily unionized states. This reduces competition and protects established jobs. An ever-higher federal minimum wage is an allied political device to reduce the wage advantage of Southern states, at least insofar as it applies to industry and agriculture.[12] (Regional competitive effects of coverage of retail, household, and government workers are smaller, although adverse effects, especially on teen-agers, are substantial.)[13]

The desire of unions to block any out-migration of their jobs is understandable. It is not easy on workers in a Philadelphia apparel plant

[10] Lloyd Shearer, *Parade*, February 13, 1977. The article uses material published recently in *The Vanderbilt Journal of Transnational Law*, written by Paul S. Dempsey.

[11] For a brief discussion of American multinational companies and foreign investment in the United States see M. R. Colberg, D. R. Forbush, and G. R. Whitaker, *Business Economics: Principles and Cases* (Homewood: Richard D. Irwin, Inc., 1975), Chapter 16.

[12] See, for example, M. R. Colberg, "Minimum Wage Legislation and Florida's Economic Development," *Journal of Law and Economics*, October, 1960.

[13] Yale Brozen, "The Effect of Statutory Minimum Wage Increases on Teen-Age Employment," *Journal of Law and Economics*, April, 1969 and Walter E. Williams, "Government Sanctioned Restraints That Reduce Economic Opportunities for Minorities," *Policy Review*, Fall 1977.

when the plant moves to Mississippi. However, from the perspective of competitive promotion of economic growth, higher real income, and fuller employment, the choice is between cartels and competition as the prime power in allocating scarce resources among regions.

Impact on Consumers

In order to estimate the effects that repeal of Section 14(b) would have on consumers, the present study concentrates on the textile and food industries of the present Right-to-Work states. The estimates are based chiefly on data presented in Chapter Three.

It is important to distinguish between changes in relative prices and changes in the price level of goods in general. The calculations made in this study pertain to an increase in prices of particular commodities—especially food and clothing. There is reason to believe that prices of other commodities would not decline to offset the increases in these important cost-of-living components. In addition, higher production costs in the highly competitive industries represented would be reflected in a reduced physical volume of sales. Some unemployment would result therefore in these industries. In order to alter this result, the Federal Reserve System would increase the money supply and expand credit. The commercial banking system and Federal Reserve System would thus validate the higher specific production costs and product prices, thereby stimulating inflation and reducing the relative purchasing power of the dollar.[14]

Other forces increasing the family budget would also result from the repeal of Section 14(b). Both firms and unions adversely affected by increased competition from imports would lobby for higher tariffs and/or lower quotas on imported apparel, food products, furniture, shoes, and other items. To the extent that such efforts are successful, consumers pay the bill.

Public-sector labor organization, already the fastest growing sector, would undoubtedly be stimulated by repeal of 14(b). In their role as taxpayers, consumers would pay the higher salaries brought about by larger public-sector unionism. A further upward push on tax rates would be felt to the extent that increased unionism affected minimum

---

[14] This idea has been forcefully stated by Friedrich A. von Hayek, a 1974 Nobel Prize Laureate, in *The Constitution of Liberty* (Chicago: University of Chicago Press, 1960) page 281:

> The process is sometimes described as though wage increases directly produced inflation. This is not correct. If the supply of money and credit were not expanded, the wage increases would rapidly lead to unemployment. But under the influence of a doctrine that represents it as the duty of the monetary authorities to provide enough money to secure full employment at any given wage level, it is politically inevitable that each round of wage increases should lead to further inflation.

pay on public works projects. The Davis-Bacon Act ties such minima to prevailing wage rates in the immediate area. This special type of federal minimum wage is likely to take on much greater importance in the coming months and years as public employment projects are put into effect by the new federal administration. The present study concentrates on the private sector and does not attempt a substantial appraisal of the very important field of public-sector unionism.

Summary

Changes in public policy cause some individuals to gain and others to lose. Unfortunately, the question is usually not only one of income redistribution since losses can easily outweigh gains in the total. If Section 14(b) were repealed, a "deadweight loss" to the economy can be anticipated. Not only will the division of the pie be altered, but the total pie will be smaller due to a poorer allocation of resources.

3

Statistical Analysis of the Impact of Repeal

In order to gain a picture of the economic position of the Right-to-Work states and some probable consequences if Section 14(b) of the Taft-Hartley Act were repealed, it is useful to have both general and detailed information about these states. This chapter will first give some of the broader data.

Population Changes

An outstanding fact of the present decade is the relative shift of population to the Southern, Mountain, and Pacific states. More than thirty percent of the net population gain came in the South Atlantic states. This shift is shown in Table 3.1 for the period April 1, 1970 to July 1, 1976.

TABLE 3.1

Population Changes, April 1, 1970–July 1, 1976

Section	Increase	Percent Increase
United States—Total	*11,354,000*	*5.6*
Northeast	443,000	0.9
North Central	1,146,000	2.0
South	6,042,000	9.6
West	3,724,000	10.7

Source: *Current Population Reports*, December 1976, U.S. Department of Commerce, Bureau of the Census.

Although the states with the largest absolute populations do not have Right-to-Work laws, the recent shift of population has been heavily toward states with these laws. While cause and effect is not entirely clear, it is likely that legislatures in the rapidly gaining states have passed Right-to-Work laws in part to keep more employment opportunities open to newcomers and that industry and population have been attracted to these less unionized states.

Table 3.2 shows the April 1, 1970 to July 1, 1976 population gains in nineteen Right-to-Work states.[15] These states accounted for about 55% of the national population increase. Proportionally, all of the Southern states with Right-to-Work laws grew faster than did the United States as a whole. Louisiana, which had no Right-to-Work law during this period, grew more slowly (5.4%) than the national average.

TABLE 3.2

Population Changes April 1, 1970–July 1, 1976
Nineteen Right-to-Work States

State	Increase	Percent Increase
Total	*6,216,000*	*10.7*
Alabama	221,000	6.4
Arizona	495,000	27.9
Arkansas	186,000	9.7
Florida	1,629,000	24.0
Georgia	382,000	8.3
Iowa	44,000	1.6
Kansas	61,000	2.7
Mississippi	137,000	6.2
Nebraska	68,000	4.5
Nevada	121,000	24.8
North Carolina	385,000	7.6
North Dakota	26,000	4.1
South Carolina	257,000	9.9
South Dakota	20,000	3.0
Tennessee	288,000	7.3
Texas	1,288,000	11.5
Utah	169,000	15.9
Virginia	381,000	8.2
Wyoming	58,000	17.4

Source: *Current Population Reports, December 1976*. U.S. Department of Commerce, Bureau of the Census.

Unionism

The extent of labor organization is below the national average in all of the first nineteen Right-to-Work states except Nevada. Proportions of non-farm workers in unions in 1972 are shown in Table 3.3. The extent of organization of non-farm workers in the Right-to-Work states runs about half as high as in the large Northern states, for which data are shown in Table 3.4.

Wage Differentials

Both dollar and real wages of American workers rise over time with technological progress, capital accumulation, and skill improvement,

[15] Louisiana, the twentieth Right-to-Work state as of July 1976, is omitted from many of the tables because any effects of this new law do not yet appear in available data.

TABLE 3.3

Organization of Non-Farm Workers
U.S. and Right-to-Work States 1972

	% of Non-Farm Workers in Unions
U.S. Total	*27.2*
Alabama	19.2
Arizona	16.6
Arkansas	16.4
Florida	14.7
Georgia	13.9
Iowa	20.0
Kansas	15.4
Mississippi	12.6
Nebraska	17.0
Nevada	33.6
North Carolina	7.5
North Dakota	16.1
South Carolina	9.0
South Dakota	11.8
Tennessee	18.4
Texas	13.5
Utah	19.4
Virginia	15.5
Wyoming	18.5

Source: *Statistical Abstract of the United States, 1975*. U.S. Department of Commerce, Bureau of the Census.

whether workers are organized to bargain collectively or are hired in competitive labor markets. Wage rates for similarly skilled persons vary, and should vary, between regions and between urban and rural locations within any region. Cost of living varies from place to place; non-pecuniary attractions such as good climate are significant, and unfavorable factors such as congestion and crime also affect the supply-demand situation and hence affect the wage rates. When industry-wide collective bargaining imposes identical money wage rates on regions with different living costs and non-pecuniary attractions, it actually

TABLE 3.4

Organization of Non-Farm Workers
Large Northern States

	% of Non-Farm Workers in Unions
Michigan	38.4
New York	38.0
Pennsylvania	37.5
Illinois	34.9
Indiana	33.2
Ohio	33.2

Source: *Business Week*, May 17, 1976. Special Report.

brings real wages to a higher level in those areas where competitive nominal wage rates would have been lower.

An especially careful study of union and non-union wage rates has been reported in the *Monthly Labor Review*.[16] The author of the study employed the concept "usual hourly earnings" which are not affected by strikes, illness, or overtime. He controlled earnings by region for union membership, age, education, and occupation. This should make the comparisons more valid than those commonly presented. Table 3.5 shows the results of the study.

TABLE 3.5

Union/Non-Union Differentials in Usual Hourly Earnings, by Region, 1974

			Excess of Union Earnings	
Region	Union	Non-Union	Dollars	Percentage
New England	$4.62	$4.41	$.21	4.8%
Middle Atlantic	4.80	4.61	.19	4.0%
East North Central	5.04	4.49	.55	12.2%
West North Central	4.87	3.99	.88	22.0%
South Atlantic	4.71	4.06	.65	16.0%
East South Central	4.48	3.72	.76	20.4%
West South Central	4.53	3.83	.70	18.2%
Mountain	4.84	4.11	.73	17.7%
Pacific	5.01	4.63	.38	8.2%

Source: *Monthly Labor Review*, U.S. Department of Labor, December 1974.

Five of the Southern Right-to-Work states are classified by the United States Census as being in the South Atlantic region: Virginia, North Carolina, South Carolina, Georgia, and Florida. Three are in the East South Central region: Tennessee, Alabama, and Mississippi. Three are classified as West South Central: Arkansas, Louisiana, and Texas. On the average, union wage rates (usual hourly earnings) are 19.5% above non-union rates in these three regions.

These data on earnings differences, together with Census of Manufactures information on the importance of labor costs in manufacturing, provide a basis for estimating the magnitude of price increases in industries that would probably be most affected by an invalidation of Right-to-Work laws.

Manufacturing Employment

The (nineteen) Right-to-Work states have gained quite dramatically in their share of the nation's total manufacturing employment. These

[16] Paul M. Ryscavage, "Measuring Union-Non-Union Earnings Differences," *Monthly Labor Review*, December 1974. The study covers professional, managerial, clerical, sales, craft, operative transportation equipment, laborer, and service personnel. It excludes the farm and public sectors.

TABLE 3.6

Growth of Manufacturing Employment in Right-to-Work States, 1958–1972

State	Percent of U.S. Manufacturing Employment			
	1958	1963	1967	1972
Alabama	1.43	1.44	1.49	1.70
Arizona	0.25	0.34	0.40	0.50
Arkansas	0.55	0.67	0.74	0.96
Florida	1.07	1.37	1.48	1.81
Georgia	1.96	2.09	2.19	2.46
Iowa	1.04	1.05	1.09	1.13
Kansas	0.74	0.67	0.74	0.73
Louisiana	0.85	0.78	0.85	0.95
Mississippi	0.68	0.76	0.83	1.06
Nebraska	0.37	0.38	0.40	0.45
Nevada	0.03	0.04	0.04	0.04
North Carolina	2.88	3.13	3.33	3.93
North Dakota	0.04	0.04	0.04	0.05
South Carolina	1.41	1.54	1.57	1.82
South Dakota	0.08	0.08	0.08	0.09
Tennessee	1.74	1.97	2.16	2.47
Texas	2.98	3.03	3.40	3.87
Utah	0.23	0.32	0.24	0.30
Virginia	1.61	1.78	1.76	1.98
Wyoming	0.04	0.04	0.03	0.03
Total (excluding Louisiana)	19.13	20.74	22.01	25.38

Source: *U.S. Census of Manufactures, 1972, Area Reports.* U.S. Department of Commerce, Bureau of the Census.

percentages are shown in Table 3.6. Between the 1958 and 1972 U.S. Census of Manufactures, the nineteen states increased their proportion from 19.13% to 25.38%. North Carolina, Texas, Florida, and Tennessee made especially impressive gains. Some of the other states such as Arizona and Arkansas, starting from smaller bases, grew even more rapidly. Louisiana made the poorest showing among Southern states with no gain between 1958 and 1967 and a moderate one between 1967 and 1972. It is not surprising that the legislature passed a Right-to-Work law in 1976 in an attempt to make the state more attractive to new plants.

Since the data of Table 3.6 are on a percentage basis, they imply a relative reduction of manufacturing employment in the non-Right-to-Work states as a whole. Some illustrative declines are: Ohio, 7.50% to 7.12% between 1958 and 1972; Pennsylvania, 8.15% to 7.48%; Massachusetts, 4.25% to 3.31%; West Virginia, 0.73% to 0.63%; New Jersey, 4.96% to 4.41%; and Washington, 1.34% to 1.19%. It is not suggested that declines were registered by all non-Right-to-Work states, however.

Rankings of the twenty Right-to-Work states in value of manufac-

TABLE 3.7

Ranking of Right-to-Work States in Value of Shipments of Manufactured Goods, 1972

Rank	State	Value of Shipments (mil. $)
1	Texas	$36,628.9
2	North Carolina	24,123.0
3	Georgia	18,360.3
4	Tennessee	16,150.9
5	Virginia	12,825.3
6	Florida	11,959.3
7	Louisiana	11,290.2
8	Alabama	11,241.2
9	South Carolina	10,726.8
10	Kansas	8,061.5
11	Iowa	7,947.0
12	Mississippi	6,539.0
13	Arkansas	6,519.9
14	Nebraska	5,898.4
15	Arizona	4,041.2
16	Utah	2,619.6
17	South Dakota	936.6
18	North Dakota	593.9
19	Wyoming	452.6
20	Nevada	423.4

Source: *U.S. Census of Manufactures, 1972, Area Reports.* U.S. Department of Commerce, Bureau of the Census.

tured products shipped from factories are given in Table 3.7. Texas, North Carolina, Georgia, and Tennessee led in 1972. These values include the cost of incorporated materials which boosts the showing of Texas because of the high value of crude oil.

An approach that eliminates the cost of materials is "value added by manufacture." A shortcoming of the U.S. Census of Manufactures data on value added is that it classifies as "production workers" many professional persons such as engineers and managers whose contribution is more nearly that of "human capital" than "labor." Unionization of such professional people is less likely to occur than it is for the presently non-unionized skilled, semi-skilled, and unskilled workers. The contribution of professionals to value added by manufacture varies considerably from industry to industry and to a lesser degree for the same two-digit industry between states. ("Transportation equipment," for example, may include aircraft and automobiles in one state and consist mainly of trailers in another.) Table 3.8 shows these estimated average contributions to value added by manufacture in 1958.

For each of the nineteen states with Right-to-Work laws in 1972, Table 3.9 shows the three leading industries in value added by manufacture, the amount of such value, and the calculated dollar contribution of professionals and other workers to value added. Also, the percent added by labor (other workers) gives a measure of labor intensiveness of each of these important industries (two-digit classification). The value added by professionals and other workers does not equal total value added as the contribution made by material capital is not shown directly.

It can be seen in Table 3.9 that North Carolina, South Carolina, Georgia, and Alabama lead in importance of textiles production. Food products are a leading industry in many states, with Texas, Iowa, Florida, and Georgia leading among the Right-to-Work states. In view of the great importance of food in the family budget, it is clear that an increase in the extent of labor organization in this industry would have an important impact on the cost of living.

It can also be seen in Table 3.9 that the textile industry is about twice as labor intensive as food products manufacturing, with approximately 44% on the average contributed to value of manufacture by labor compared with about 22% for food products. (These contributions are measured by the payroll for production workers, after deduction of estimated pay to professional persons in the factories.) Although clothing

TABLE 3.8

Contribution of Professional Persons to Value Added by Manufacture in the South, 1958

Industry	Percentage of Value Added by Professionals
Machinery, except electrical	17.4
Transportation equipment	13.8
Fabricated metal products	13.6
Petroleum products	8.9
Electrical machinery	8.7
Chemicals and allied products	8.3
Food products	8.1
Rubber and plastic products	7.8
Stone, clay and glass products	7.2
Primary metals	6.9
Furniture and fixtures	6.1
Paper and allied products	5.9
Leather products	5.3
Apparel	4.2
Textiles	3.8
Tobacco products	2.4

Source: Marshall R. Colberg, *Human Capital in Southern Development: 1939–1963.* (Chapel Hill: University of North Carolina Press, 1965), p. 88. The estimated contributions of professionals were compiled by a process involving matching of the 1958 Census of Manufactures and the 1960 Census of Population (actually pertaining to 1959). It is believed, however, that when utilized in conjunction with the 1972 Census of Manufactures, the estimates will assist in making a better measurement of the value added.

TABLE 3.9

Contributions to Value Added by Manufacturing, Three Leading Industries, Right-to-Work States, 1972

State and Industry	Value Added by Manufacture (mil. $) By Professionals	By other Workers	Total	Percent Added by Labor (other workers)
Alabama				
Primary metals	17.3	335.0	806.1	42
Paper & products	8.0	124.9	468.8	27
Textiles	6.8	213.4	457.4	47
Arizona				
Electrical equipment	7.9	83.2	331.8	25
Primary metals	4.1	55.3	310.0	18
Machinery, ex. electrical	7.7	36.8	309.1	12
Arkansas				
Food products	8.0	91.6	363.3	25
Electrical equipment	7.9	83.0	340.3	24
Lumber	5.3	101.5	270.3	37
Florida				
Food products	16.0	181.2	968.7	19
Transportation equipment	7.0	176.6	700.2	25
Electrical equipment	11.7	123.2	580.9	21
Georgia				
Textiles	23.9	546.3	1,565.9	35
Transportation equipment	32.0	210.7	901.6	23
Food products	16.1	169.4	832.0	20
Iowa				
Machinery, ex. electrical	64.9	307.9	1,204.2	26
Food products	27.1	307.3	1,112.0	28
Electrical equipment	9.7	101.4	405.3	25
Kansas				
Transportation equipment	28.4	177.6	684.0	26
Food products	8.2	93.0	437.9	21
Machinery, ex. electrical	18.4	87.2	328.7	26
Mississippi				
Lumber	5.4	103.6	292.2	35
Apparel	4.5	133.2	274.3	49
Transportation equipment	13.0	143.8	267.8	54
Nebraska				
Food products	12.4	140.9	581.0	24
Machinery, ex. electrical	8.9	42.2	192.2	22
Electrical equipment	4.6	48.6	171.6	28
Nevada				
Stone, clay, and glass products	0.8	10.2	35.8	28
Chemical and allied products	0.5	5.0	35.5	14
Food products	0.4	5.1	30.0	17

TABLE 3.9 (Continued)

Contributions to Value Added by Manufacturing, Three Leading Industries, Right-to-Work States, 1972

State and Industry	Value Added by Manufacture (mil. $) By Professionals	By other Workers	Total	Percent Added by Labor (other workers)
North Carolina				
Textiles	53.4	1,282.6	3,008.5	42
Tobacco products	3.9	152.7	1,263.8	12
Chemicals and allied products	11.9	131.3	887.0	15
North Dakota				
Food products	1.3	14.4	66.9	22
Machinery, ex. electrical	1.6	7.7	39.6	20
Stone, clay, and glass products	0.2	2.0	5.2	39
South Carolina				
Textiles	25.6	750.9	1,725.9	44
Chemicals and allied products	10.9	144.3	813.7	18
Machinery, ex. electrical	16.4	77.8	406.4	19
South Dakota				
Food products	3.7	42.3	127.0	33
Machinery, ex. electrical	1.7	8.2	39.8	21
Lumber	0.4	7.1	23.8	30
Tennessee				
Chemicals and allied products	24.2	267.4	1,396.0	19
Electrical equipment	9.5	156.9	692.2	23
Food products	11.6	131.0	690.2	19
Texas				
Chemicals and allied products	19.1	355.5	3,189.8	11
Food products	25.9	293.5	1,716.6	17
Machinery, ex. electrical	68.9	327.0	1,449.9	23
Utah				
Transportation equipment	3.5	22.2	151.0	15
Food products	2.3	26.7	142.9	19
Machinery, ex. electrical	5.2	24.7	115.9	21
Virginia				
Chemicals and allied products	16.4	180.8	844.4	21
Food products	9.9	120.8	610.7	21
Electrical equipment	22.3	99.5	557.5	18
Wyoming				
Petroleum products	1.0	10.3	53.0	20
Stone, clay, and glass products	0.5	6.0	21.7	28
Food products	0.4	5.0	19.4	26

Sources: *U.S. Census of Manfactures, 1972* and Marshall R. Colberg, *Human Capital in Southern Development, 1939–1963.*

is less important than food in the family budget, the great reliance on Right-to-Work states for textile output and the high importance of labor costs in the industry make the consumer impact of any repeal of Right-to-Work laws potentially substantial.

Estimating Price Increases

Estimating the quantitative impact of invalidation of the Right-to-Work laws is necessarily imprecise although the general directions of resulting price changes are not difficult to anticipate. In the following pages, estimates are based on the following assumptions:

1) The Right-to-Work laws are important since for many years they have been the subject of strong debate and vigorous legislative efforts by both sides.
2) If Section 14(b) were repealed, a significant boost would be given to the principle of the compulsory union shop with the result that substantial unionization would occur in the textile and food products industries of present Right-to-Work states.
3) The extent of unionization of these industries would be sufficient to raise production workers' wage rates to the present level of pay of unionized workers in the same regions of the country. This would mean about a 20% increase in wage rates.
4) The calculated degree of labor intensiveness of manufacturing also applies, by state, to the associated material producing activities. For example, the cotton ginning process is assumed to be as labor intensive as the cotton textile industry of the same state.
5) There would be induced inflation rather than just an increase in food and textile prices and an off-setting decrease in other prices, with the likely result of layoffs in the textile, food products, furniture, and other affected industries.

The use of some of these assumptions can be traced in Tables 3.10 and 3.11 where price increases for textiles and food products, respectively, are estimated. These price increases are estimated to be 8% for textiles and 4.3% for food. The classification "textile mill products" as used by the Department of Commerce actually includes a great deal of wearing apparel since the same mills often knit final products from their own yarn or fabrics such as women's hosiery and pantyhose, children's anklets, men's sportshirts, sweaters, jackets, and underwear. Consequently, it is reasonable to use the estimated price increase for textile mills that would be occasioned by unionism as an estimated increase in clothing prices.

Because of the great importance of the Southern textile industry it is estimated that three quarters of the items in the average clothing budget would be affected by this 8% price increase. Additionally, food

TABLE 3.10

Textiles—Estimate of Price Increase if Industry Unionized

Leading States	Value of Shipments (mil. $) 1972	Cost of Materials (mil. $) 1972	Estimated Percent Due to Labor	Material Cost Due to Labor	Value Added to Mfr. by Labor
	(1)	(2)	(3)	(2)×(3)	Table 3.9
Alabama	1,128.0	671.4	47%	315.6	213.4
Georgia	4,013.1	2,481.0	35	868.4	546.3
North Carolina	7,541.5	4,566.5	42	1,917.9	1,282.6
South Carolina	4,285.5	2,578.8	44	1,134.7	750.9
Totals	16,968.1	10,297.7		4,236.6	2,793.2

Estimated Added Materials Cost if Unionized	4,236.6 × 20% = $847.3 mil
Estimated Added Manufacturing Cost if Unionized	2,793.2 × 20% = $558.6 mil
Estimated Total Added Cost	$1,405.9 mil

Value of 1972 Shipments	$16,968.1 mil
Added Value if Quantity Same	1,405.9 mil

Percent increase in Price $\frac{1{,}405.9}{16{,}968.1} = 8\%$

TABLE 3.11

Food Products—Estimate of Price Increase if Industry Unionized

Leading States	Value of Shipments (mil. $) 1972	Cost of Materials (mil. $) 1972	Estimated Percent Due to Labor	Material Cost Due to Labor	Value Added to Mfr. by Labor
	(1)	(2)	(3)	(2)×(3)	Table 3.9
Florida	3,020.2	2,071.2	19	393.5	181.2
Georgia	2,640.0	1,821.7	20	364.3	169.4
Iowa	5,829.0	4,737.5	28	1,326.5	307.3
Texas	5,573.1	3,881.9	17	659.9	293.5
Totals	17,062.3	12,512.3		2,744.2	951.4

Estimated Added Materials Cost if Unionized	2,744.2 × 20% = $548.8 mil
Estimated Added Manufacturing Cost if Unionized	951.4 × 20% = 190.3 mil
Estimated Total Added Cost	739.1 mil

Value of 1972 Shipments	$17,062.3 mil
Added Value if Quantity Same	739.1 mil

Percent increase in price $\frac{739.1}{17{,}062.3} = 4.3\%$

products are produced in all states; but in view of the great agricultural importance of Iowa, a Right-to-Work state, it is reasonable to assume that half the food budget of an average family would be affected by the estimated 4.3% increase in food prices.

Table 3.12 shows a U.S. government statement of an annual budget for a four-person family at the intermediate income level as of Autumn 1975. According to the estimates made in the present study, this food budget would rise by $82 per year and the clothing budget by $86 per year. The cost of furniture would rise to some extent since the entire wood products industry in the Right-to-Work states is lightly unionized. In the Right-to-Work states themselves there would be an increase in the cost of residential construction.

TABLE 3.12

Annual Budget for a Four-person Family Intermediate Level, Autumn 1975

			Percent of Total
Total Cost		$15,318	100.0%
Total Consumption		11,725	76.5
Food	$3,827		25.0
Housing	3,533		23.1
Transportation	1,279		8.3
Clothing, personal care	1,433		9.4
Medical care	822		5.4
Other	831		5.4
Other items		702	4.7
Social Security		834	5.4
Personal Income Taxes		2,057	13.4

Source: *Statistical Abstract of the United States, 1976*. U.S. Department of Commerce, Bureau of the Census.

If Section 14(b) of the Taft-Hartley Act were repealed and assuming rapid unionization in present Right-to-Work states, an estimated increase in the typical family budget in the neighborhood of $200 per year is anticipated. The estimated increase of $200 is likely to be low; stronger labor organization in the textile and food industry is likely to be accompanied by a strong political effort on the part of both the companies and the unions to reduce imports of foreign-made apparel and food products. This would tend further to increase prices for domestic food and apparel.

Finally, a repeal of state Right-to-Work laws would encourage unionism among employees in all other sectors, including the public sector, at the expense of consumers as taxpayers.

Appendix:

Economic Profiles of the Right-to-Work States

A brief sketch of the economy of each of the twenty states that currently has Right-to-Work laws is included in this appendix.

Sources for these data include heavy reliance on the excellent and comprehensive volume by Donald J. Bogue and Calvin L. Beale, *Economic Areas of the United States* (New York: The Free Press of Glencoe, 1961); census reports of the Department of Commerce; *The Statistical Abstract of the United States*; Department of Labor reports; and trade magazines and books previously cited. Where data were previously cited, as in Chapter 3, sources are not repeated.

Arizona

Arizona was one of the earliest Right-to-Work states, passing a constitutional amendment with voluntary union provisions even before passage of the Taft-Hartley Act. The State also has the distinction of growing at the most rapid rate since 1970 (although achievement of a high growth rate is easier when the base is low). Arizona's percentage of national manufacturing employment doubled between 1958 and 1972 (0.25 to 0.50 percent). Manufacturing is less labor intensive than in the more typical Right-to-Work states in the South.

Southern Arizona is the rapid growth area, with Maricopa County, containing Phoenix, having about half of the total state population. Irrigation has made possible a flourishing agricultural area in the vicinity of Phoenix. Maricopa County ranked fifth in the nation in 1960 in total value of farm products sold.[1] These include cotton, citrus fruit, dates, nuts, truck crops, and cattle feed. For the state as a whole cotton, hay, lettuce, and wheat had the largest value in 1973.[2]

Maricopa County, which comprises the Phoenix Standard Metropolitan Area, also has such fast-growing cities as Mesa, Tempe, Glendale, and Scottsdale. The Phoenix area employs thousands of workers

[1] Bogue and Beale, p. 528. Other detailed information is also from this source.

[2] *Statistical Abstract of the United States*, 1975.

in the production of aircraft parts, extruded aluminum, electronic products, coolers, clothing and other goods. The dry climate, with hot days and cool nights, has brought many residents and has attracted hospitals and other health institutions.

Among the Right-to-Work states, Arizona was second only to Texas in mineral production in 1973. Copper, molybdenum, sand and gravel, and portland cement were the leaders. Copper is mined heavily in the Southeastern part of Arizona. Crop farming is limited in the Southeastern counties by lack of water but livestock farming is quite important.

Tucson, about 125 miles Southeast of Phoenix, is growing rapidly. In addition to health-related facilities, Tucson has acquired aircraft and missile plants since the Korean War. The University of Arizona and a large air base add importantly to activity in the area.

Alabama

Alabama has a relatively high percentage of non-farm labor organization (19.2 percent in 1972) for a Right-to-Work state. This is due to unionism in the Birmingham district where some thirty thousand persons work in the blast furnaces, mills, and foundries and about two thirds as many work in nearby mines and in transportation.

To the North, near the Tennessee border, the main crop historically has been cotton, and it is still important. (For the State, as a whole, soybeans, cotton, corn, and peanuts are the leading crops.) The Northern counties in Alabama have an important advantage in the low cost electric power generated by the TVA system. Near the Northwest corner of Alabama, Florence, Sheffield, Tuscumbia, and Muscle Shoals are located just below Wilson Dam. Aluminum and metal products are important manufactures. A long-established cotton textile industry provides substantial private employment around Huntsville but the Redstone Arsenal provides larger public employment and makes Huntsville a very high per capita income town.

A little farther South, Gadsden and Anniston are important industrial cities that have grown rapidly during the twentieth century. Gadsden establishments include a steel mill, a tire factory, and a cotton textile mill. Anniston has textile plants and foundries making cast iron pipe. Two smaller towns in the general area, Talladega and Sylacauga, are textile centers.

For Alabama as a whole, textiles rank third in amount of value added by manufacture, behind primary metals and paper and allied products. A large newsprint plant on the Coosa River contributes to the latter industry. The Alabama textile industry is larger than that of Mississippi but well behind North Carolina, South Carolina and Georgia in size.

Toward the South of the State, the capital, Montgomery, is located in one of the best farming regions. Government and other non-manufacturing activities predominate. However, a number of relatively small plants turn out furniture, food products, building materials, textiles and apparel.

Mobile, a port on the Gulf of Mexico, has developed a large chemical industry in recent decades. Large scale production of alumina and paper is of great economic consequence. Civilian and military employment by the federal government is large, and government-supported marine research is carried on at nearby Dauphin Island.

Commercial timberland covers nearly 22 million acres, second in the South only to Georgia. About one fourth of the population of Alabama is Black. Only Mississippi and South Carolina have larger proportions of non-white inhabitants. Georgia is close to Alabama in this respect.

Arkansas

Arkansas is an especially rural state. It has experienced the typical Southern decline in cotton output and substitution of soybean, poultry, livestock, timber and industrial production. Cotton is now third in value as an agricultural crop, behind soybeans and rice. Ashley and Drew counties in Southeast Arkansas are extremely productive in cotton and rice.

In mineral production the state is rather fortunate, with petroleum, bromine, natural gas, and portland cement being valued at over a quarter billion dollars in output in 1973. The only large domestic source of bauxite is found in central Arkansas. Near the mines are alumina plants and an aluminum reduction mill.

Little Rock, in the center of the State, is the dominant city in population, manufacturing, wholesale and retail trade, and transportation. Unlike many regions of the State, the Little Rock area has expanded rapidly in population. Arkansas as a whole lost population between 1950 and 1960, but gained a substantial 9.7 percent in number of inhabitants between April 1, 1970, and July 1, 1976.

Manufacturing employment as a proportion of the nation's total has expanded steadily, although it is not high in absolute level. In 1958 the percentage was 0.55; in 1963, 0.67; 1967, 0.74; and 1972, 0.96. Food products, electrical equipment, and lumber led in value added by manufacture in 1972. Rapid growth industries include leather, paper, furniture, apparel, and chemicals.

Fort Smith, near the Oklahoma border, is an important producer of household furniture. The city is a trading center for the general area and, in addition to wood products, houses the manufacture of glass, canned goods, paper cups, and metal products.

Hot Springs is quite different in nature, being primarily a recreational, tourist, and convention center. It was designated a federal reservation in 1832 in order to control the use of the 47 thermal springs located there.

Florida

Florida has long been a leader in opposing monopolistic practices, being the first state to find a Fair Trade Law unconstitutional and the first to pass a Right-to-Work law (in the form of a constitutional amendment).

Although the rate of population growth seems to be diminishing, Florida had a net increase of 1,629,000 persons between April 1, 1970, and July 1, 1976, according to Census estimates. This 24 percent increase was exceeded slightly by two other Right-to-Work states, Arizona and Nevada.

The Florida economy is heavily dependent on tourism, citrus production, sugarcane, livestock, manufacturing, construction, fishing, and winter vegetables. The January 1977 heavy freeze was disastrous to the winter vegetable crop and to the army of migrant workers who were ready to harvest the crops. Repercussions will be felt by workers and owners of food products plants which in the manufacturing process normally add almost a billion dollars per year in value to citrus, vegetables, and other material inputs.

Miami and Miami Beach have grown rapidly in population with the development of tourism, retirement, international air travel, and nearby agriculture. In recent decades the city had had a very large influx of former residents of Cuba. Construction, manufacturing and financial services have been attracted by and have contributed to the rapid growth. Much of the manufacturing is demand-oriented such as style goods, aluminum furniture, boats, swimming pools, and food products.

Orlando, in Central Florida, is a city of rapid growth, stimulated in recent years by the large nearby Disneyworld complex. Aircraft and missile production are important, relatively new, activities. Located in a large citrus-producing area, Orlando is a major packing, canning, and shipment center for these products.

Across the State, Tampa and St. Petersburg provide industrial and retirement activities, the former being mainly in Tampa. Phosphate, by far Florida's leading mineral product, is exported largely from Tampa. St. Petersburg has attracted important electronic and other technical products, manufacturing and research facilities in part because of the availability of retired engineers from all parts of the nation.

Jacksonville is the major port on the Atlantic Ocean south of Norfolk.

In addition to import and export activities there is automobile assembly, paper production, chemical, and food products production.

The chemical industry, and its related products such as nylon, has become very important in the Western Florida coastal area around Pensacola. Unfortunately, air and water pollution are accompanying "bads." Northwest Florida also features excellent beaches patronized heavily by Southerners. Pine forests and extensive military bases are other features. The capital, Tallahassee, about halfway between St. Augustine and Pensacola, has two State Universities in addition to large government office buildings.

In relation to the nation's total manufacturing employment, Florida had 1.07 percent in 1958 and 1.81 percent in 1972—one of the more rapid increases.

Georgia

Georgia's economy is well-diversified, including automobile assembly, airplane production, cattle raising, broiler production, corn, peanuts, soybeans, cotton, textiles, more commercial timberland than any other state, and an important new product—national political leadership. Its largest city, Atlanta, has a higher elevation (1,050 feet above sea level) than does any other city of comparable size in the eastern half of the nation.[3] This contributes to a summer climate that is more favorable than that of most Southern cities. Atlanta is a transportation and communications center, a wholesaling and distribution center, and a convention center with modern hotels.

Although Atlanta has important textile plants these do not dominate its manufacturing activity. For the State as a whole, however, the textile industry has the greatest value added by manufacturing, with transportation equipment and food products following.

Cotton growing has declined sharply in Georgia, often being replaced by poultry raising, cattle production, or pine forests. Cotton was replaced to an especially large degree in the upper part of Southwest Georgia by large-scale production of peanuts, including that near Plains in Sumter County. Livestock, cash grain, and peaches are also important agricultural crops. Farther to the South, reaching to the Florida border, a well-diversified agriculture includes tobacco, cotton, hogs, vegetables, cattle, cash grain, milk, eggs and chickens.

In Northwest Georgia manufacturing is more important than agriculture as an income source. Textiles lead, with tufted textiles (chenille goods) being the best known items. As in other parts of the State, many

---

[3] Bogue and Beale, p. 614. Other detailed information is mainly from this source.

former cotton farmers have turned to poultry, livestock, and dairy products.

Columbus on the Alabama border is the largest textile mill center in Georgia. Food products, especially candy, are second in importance. The candy makers utilize large quantities of peanuts from the nearby peanut belt. Fort Benning, with its large payroll, is of great importance to Columbus and the adjacent area, including Phenix City, directly across the Chattahoochee River in Alabama.

Augusta and Savannah are important cities near the South Carolina border. Textiles are important in Augusta, but do not dominate the industrial base which also includes brick and tile, lumber, cottonseed oil, and foods. Camp Gordon adds importantly to the economic base. Savannah, to the Southeast, depends heavily on the activity of its seaport. Wood and paper products, chemicals and chemical products are important manufactures.

Macon, in the very center of Georgia, is not a major textile town but has production of clothing, coarse yarns, and fabric. Naval ordnance clay products, and pulp and paper goods such as insulation material are substantial manufactures. The Warner Robins airbase and maintenance facilities is an important economic factor in the Macon area.

The extent of union organization among non-farm workers (13.9 percent in 1972) is about average for Southern Right-to-Work states. In contrast, the large Northern industrial states averaged about 35 percent in union organization. While relative manufacturing employment has declined in the Northern states, Georgia's increased from 1.96 to 2.46 percent of the national total between the 1958 and 1972 Censuses of Manufactures.

Iowa

Blessed with a great deal of excellent farmland, Iowa is the leading producer of food products among the twenty Right-to-Work states. Second only to California, Iowa produced crops worth over five billion dollars in 1974. In manufacturing the state ranks just below the middle among Right-to-Work states. Timber and mineral production are relatively unimportant although there is some coal in several South Central counties.

Northwestern Iowa is sometimes called the "western meat area," having one of the world's highest outputs of meat per square mile. Corn is *the* crop in this part of the state. Oats are also important, although for Iowa as a whole corn, soybeans, and hay lead oats in value. Both cattle and hog raising takes place on a large scale. Southwestern Iowa is quite similar, although the land is somewhat poorer and is devoted more to livestock. Many small canning factories, located so as to be near the crops, are active in Western Iowa.

Central Iowa is often called the "Central Grain area." The level land is ideal for tractor use. Soybeans are second only to corn as a cash crop to the farmers, many of whom are tenants rather than owners, since outsiders have considered Iowa farm land to be a good investment. Near Des Moines a dairy industry serves the urban population. To the Southeast of Des Moines, Ottumwa is the location of farm machinery production, which tends to take place in the farming areas of the country because it is too bulky to be cheaply transported long distances. In the 1972 Census of Manufactures, "machinery, except electrical" exceeded even food products in value added by manufacture.

Northeastern Iowa is often called the "Iowa Dairy area" although meat production is even more important. The land is not so rich as it is to the West.

Along the Mississippi River, Eastern Iowa is quite urban, and the cities have had a long history because of the early importance of river transportation. Dubuque is a relatively large town where wood products are important along with farm machinery, meat packing, and food processing. It also serves as a wholesaling, shopping, and marketing center. Burlington, also on the river, has diversified manufacturing, including electrical equipment, wood products, machinery, and chemicals. Muscatine, in addition to more conventional products, produces pearl buttons from fresh water mussels.

Davenport in Iowa, and Rock Island and Moline in Illinois, constitute a large industrial concentration on the Mississippi River. The interstate nature of air pollution has been a problem. Davenport produces a wide variety of goods including farm machinery, aluminum foil, fabricated metal products, and food products.

In Eastern Iowa, but not on the river, Cedar Rapids is the headquarters of Quaker Oats. The corn refining industry, which turns out cornstarch and corn syrup, has facilities in Cedar Rapids. Meat packing, heavy machinery, and various metal products are also turned out.

Iowa is more unionized than most of the Right-to-Work states. With 21.2 percent of non-agricultural workers organized, it compares with 26.2 percent for the nation as a whole in 1974.[4]

Kansas

Kansas is a leading agricultural state, although the value of farm crops is only about half that of Iowa. Wheat and sorghum are the lead-

[4] Source: *Statistical Abstract of the United States, 1976*, U.S. Department of Commerce, Bureau of the Census, p. 384.

ing crops. In manufacturing the state ranks about in the middle of the Right-to-Work states, with much of this output being farm-related.

In the Southwestern part of the state farms are typically of thousand acre size but moisture is often insufficient, and some of the counties were part of the "dust bowl" during the drought of 1934 to 1936. Dodge City of "Gunsmoke" fame is on the Arkansas River. Several of the counties are important producers of natural gas.

Seemingly endless fields of wheat grow in the more central counties. Many of the farms raise both wheat and cattle. Where moisture conditions are more favorable for late maturing crops, corn is raised, making it third in importance among Kansas crops. Hutchinson, in Reno County, is built over a great salt deposit, making mining, processing, and shipping of salt a principal activity. The deposits are deep, but are so thick as to be almost inexhaustible. Hutchinson is also a major wheat center. Salina, to the North, has large grain elevators and flour mills as well as meat packing. Wichita, also in the Central wheat belt, is a leading aircraft production center. A factor in this location is the favorable flying weather. Sedgwick County, in which Wichita is located, has produced oil since shortly after World War I. Petroleum and natural gas gave Kansas a high rating among the Right-to-Work states in mineral production in 1973. Flour milling, oil refining, and meat packing take place in Wichita, based on local resources.

Kansas City, Kansas, is directly across the Missouri River from Kansas City, Missouri, and many persons cross the river in both directions to work. Good railroad and water transportation has encouraged a wide variety of manufactures, including farm machinery, oil refining, and portland cement. Grain storage elevators are numerous.

Not far to the West is Topeka, the capital city. In addition to government offices, Topeka has important medical and health facilities. Its location in an especially fertile area of the state makes the city a shopping center for a prosperous rural population and a wholesaling and marketing center. Although less than 5 percent of the Kansas population is non-white, the proportion in Topeka is about 13 percent.

The degree of unionization of labor in Kansas is about comparable to the average of the Southern Right-to-Work states. Quite a substantial decline has occurred in percent of non-agricultural employees organized: 18.6 percent in 1964; 16.5 percent in 1970; and 14.1 percent in 1974.[5]

[5] *Statistical Abstract of the United States, 1976*, U.S. Department of Commerce, Bureau of the Census, p. 384.

Louisiana

Louisiana became the twentieth Right-to-Work state in July 1976 after a bitter legislative struggle. Unionization of labor in the State appears to have declined in recent years, although full information on organization is not available. Labor union membership among non-agricultural employees was 16.3 percent in 1974 compared with 18.7 percent a decade earlier.

New Orleans is a leading tourist attraction, port, commercial, industrial, and financial center. Manufacturing is highly diversified including shipbuilding and repair, food products, clothing, paper products, and oil refining. Wholesale and retail trade, medical service, and public administration are other major sectors.

Baton Rouge, the capital of Louisiana, has grown rapidly in population and importance. Oilfields and refineries in the vicinity form the industry base. Related plants of many kinds are present. Natural gas, sulphur, and limestone contribute to the chemical complex.

In the Lake Charles area to the West, oil refining and petrochemical operations flourish. Rice mills process the product of the nearby fields, where rice is the dominant crop. Urban population in the Western area has grown rapidly with the stimulus of manufacturing which has been aided also by a deepwater channel to the Gulf of Mexico.

In Northwestern Louisiana, Shreveport is the large city. Employment is large in natural gas distribution and wholesale trade. The city's remoteness from other large urban places makes it a cotton market for the fertile Red River Valley—a function that it has long performed.

North of Lake Ponchartrain lumbering and papermaking are important. Bogalusa has large pulp and paper mills. Black workers are employed in the lumber industry in greater numbers than their share of the population in the South as a whole.[6] Only the textile industry has a lower rate of unionization.

Central Louisiana still has cotton as the dominant crop. Sugarcane, sweet potatoes, and rice are other important farm products. Cattle raising, along with pecan groves and broiler chickens, add to income in this highly diversified state.

Mississippi

King Cotton has lost dominance in Mississippi's agricultural economy but is still important, being second to soybeans and ahead of rice. Large numbers of former cottonfield workers, mainly Blacks, have left the

[6] John C. Howard, "The Negro in the Lumber Industry," in H. R. Northrup and R. L. Rowan, *Negro Employment in Southern Industry* (University of Pennsylvania, Wharton School of Finance and Commerce, 1970).

state for the Northern cities. The exodus was heightened when the federal minimum wage was extended in 1967 to agriculture and many cotton root "choppers" were replaced by chemicals.[7] Still, many persons, including retired former residents, move back to Mississippi each year, attracted in part by the relatively low cost of living. A net population gain of 6.2 percent was made between April 1, 1970, and July 1, 1976.

Per capita income is low, but the state has made an unusually strong effort in its "Balance Agriculture With Industry" program to improve its economic position. With the approval of local voters, Mississippi towns issue bonds, construct and lease plants, and otherwise subsidize new firms that will locate there. Well-known firms are often attracted by these inducements—partly because of the favorable attitude toward business which they reflect. Further, the extent of labor organization is low—12.6 percent of non-farm workers in 1972. Mississippi has shown a good gain in percentage of the nation's total manufacturing employment: 0.68 percent in 1958 to 1.06 percent in 1972, according to Census of Manufactures data.

Mississippi's leading industries—lumber, apparel, and transportation equipment (mainly trailers)—are more labor-intensive than those of any other state. Economic development is being aided by oil wells and natural gas, though on a limited scale compared with some other states.

Poultry production, especially of broiler chickens, has grown rapidly in many sections of the state. Livestock and dairy farms are numerous but tend to be smaller than in other states. Commercial timberlands are extensive (almost 17 million acres in 1970) providing the material for a substantial wood products industry.

Nebraska

Nebraska ranks high among the producers of crops, processed foods, and livestock. Corn, wheat, sorghum, and hay lead the crops in value with great amounts of corn being fed to hogs. Among manufactures, food products are far in the lead (see Table 3.9) in value added. Farm machinery is second and electrical equipment third. In part the good showing in electrical equipment is due to a very large plant in Omaha that makes parts for telephones.

Northeastern Nebraska, on the western side of the Missouri River, is an especially rich farming area. Corn, oats, and hay—with corn far in the lead—are grown in these counties. Crop yields per acre are high and

[7] See Marshall R. Colberg, "Agriculture and the Minimum Wage," *Mississippi Valley Journal of Business and Economics*, Fall 1968, pp. 15-25.

corn-hog production is the outstanding characteristic. The hog and cattle population far exceed the human population.

Soil conditions are less favorable in the Southeastern counties. This is more of a "cash grain" area with less corn being fed to hogs. Livestock production is still of great importance, however.

Omaha and Lincoln are in the Southeast, the former being the largest city in the State. Located on the Missouri River, and aided by prolonged dredging of the channel, Omaha has water transportation as well as being a railroad center. Manufacturing includes food products, chemicals, clothing, machinery, and a wide variety of fabricated metal items.

Lincoln, not far to the Southwest of Omaha, is the State capital and also a university city. As in Omaha, there is manufacture of telephone equipment and food products. Lincoln is known locally as "the Hartford of the Middle West" because of the large number of insurance companies with home offices there. Like Omaha, Lincoln also has important railroad shops.

To the West the vast acreage is in large part suitable for corn, wheat, and livestock. The relative success of corn and wheat varies with soil and rainfall since corn requires more moisture.

Toward the Northwest is the Sand Hills section which covers a very large area. The soil is suitable mainly for livestock grazing. Windmills are widely used to raise water to the surface. The area is sparsely settled, but with farms of large size, irrigation, and careful management a good living can be made.

In Central Nebraska there is more urbanization, with Grand Island, Kearney, and North Platte being of substantial size. Grand Island has railroad shops and sugarbeet processing plants. North Platte is also a railroad center and marketing and distribution locale. Kearney is a commercial and college town.

Like the other Midwestern agricultural states Nebraska's population increase this decade has been modest (4.5 percent). In this respect, however, it exceeds Iowa and the Dakotas. In percent of the nation's manufacturing employment, Nebraska has risen from 0.37 percent in 1958 to 0.45 percent in 1972, according to the U.S. Census of Manufactures.

Nevada

Nevada is arid and sparsely populated but has a very rapid rate of population growth (24.8 percent from April 1, 1970, to July 1, 1976). Mineral production is substantial in value—$202 million in 1973, with copper and gold in the lead. Its principal gold mines, however, are the gambling casinos and recreation palaces of Las Vegas and Reno. These cities and their suburbs account for most of the population and the population growth.

The value of manufactured goods shipped (1972) was lowest of the twenty Right-to-Work states but was only a little below Wyoming and North Dakota. Nevada is the most unionized of the Right-to-Work states. However, the extent of non-agricultural workers organization fell from 32.5 percent in 1970 to 27.4 percent in 1974.

Agricultural output is also lowest among the Right-to-Work states with hay and alfalfa in the lead (1974). These are grown to help feed livestock in the winter months when there is a scarcity of feed on the open range.

The famous Comstock lode at Virginia City brought many of the early settlers to Nevada. It proved to be one of the richest deposits of silver and gold ever found in the West.

North Carolina

North Carolina ranks high among Southern states in education, industry, agriculture, forestry, and tourism. The growth of manufacturing has been impressive, resembling that of Texas in magnitude, though of different composition. According to the 1972 Census of Manufactures, North Carolina had 3.93 percent of the nation's manufacturing employment compared with 3.87 percent of the nation's total in Texas.[8] Since North Carolina's industry is more labor intensive, the total value added by industrial production (which includes the contribution of capital) is below that of Texas although ahead of all other Southern states.

North Carolina is by far the leader in the textile industry, where value added by manufacture in 1972 exceeded three billion dollars. Burlington Industries, largest of all textile manufacturers, has headquarters in Greensboro. (High Point, famous for its furniture, is 15 miles away.) Burlington, only twenty miles to the East, also has a concentration of yarn, fabric, and knitting mills, with heavy emphasis on hosiery. Textiles and related products are manufactured also in many other sections of the State. In the Eastern area of Central North Carolina about 60 percent of manufacturing workers are in textile and associated weaving apparel factories. In the Western area of Central North Carolina textile activity is strong in the neighboring cities of Kannapolis and Concord. Cannon Mills, the founding firm of Kannapolis, is the major manufacturer of such household items as towels, sheets, and pillowcases.[9]

[8] *U.S. Census of Manufactures, 1972, Area Statistics*, Department of Commerce, Washington, D.C.

[9] Detailed industry information is from Donald J. Bogue and Calvin L. Beale, *Economic Areas of the United States* (New York: The Free Press of Glencoe, Inc.) 1961.

Tobacco products are the second highest in value added by manufacture. Winston-Salem, the leading industrial city in North Carolina, is the foremost tobacco manufacturing center in the country. Reynolds Tobacco Company is located here. Durham factories produce about one fifth of all American cigarettes.

Tobacco is the leading agricultural crop of North Carolina, followed by corn, soybeans, and peanuts. Cotton farming has declined sharply. In value of all farm crops North Carolina led all Southern states except Texas in 1974, with output valued at about one and three quarter billion dollars.

The state also ranks high in amount of commercial timberland with over 20 million acres. Georgia and Alabama have about 25 and 22 million acres, respectively. Mineral production does not rank high in total value although many rocks are of unusual interest. The major mica and feldspar mines in the United States are in the heart of the Great Smokies country near Mt. Mitchell.

Unionization of workers is the lowest in the United States, with 7.5 percent of non-agricultural labor organized as of 1972. According to an industry source,[10] the Amalgamated Clothing and Textile Workers Union has recently abandoned efforts to organize the Cannon Mills Company in North Carolina, citing a lack of interest on the part of employees.

North Dakota

North Dakota's manufacturing is quite limited in amount and is for the most part related to its main activity, agriculture. Wheat, barley, hay, and potatoes were valued at about $1.85 billion in 1974. Mineral production is relatively low in value, with petroleum leading since the much-needed discovery of oil near Williston around 1950.

South Central North Dakota became the dumping ground of the great glaciers for boulders, making much of the land too rough to be farmed. Pasture and wild hay form the basis for livestock operations. The only sizable city, Bismarck, is a shopping, marketing, and supply center for a large but lightly populated area.

The soil is quite different in North Central North Dakota, part of the region being known as "the Black Prairie." Wheat is by far the leading crop and includes durum wheat, a distinctive type needed for macaroni and similar products. This is also a leading barley producing area. Toward the East Central section a large lake country affords recreation.

The Red River Valley along the Eastern border of the state is much more populous than other parts. Although the land is fertile and highly

[10] *Textile Industries*, November 1976, p. 11.

agricultural it also contains two substantial cities, Fargo and Grand Forks.

Fargo to the South was the entry point for the transcontinental railroad and it has maintained its lead in size over other cities. Fargo is the leading trucking, wholesaling, and financial center of the State. Grand Forks, about 60 miles to the North, has grain elevators and mills, meat packing, and other food products production.

Membership of non-agricultural workers in labor unions was a fairly low 15.1 percent in 1974—a figure that did not change much in a decade. Population grew by 4.1 percent in the six year period ending July 1, 1976. The Black population is very small in both of the Dakotas—less than one percent.

South Carolina

The long term decline in Southern cotton growing, with replacement by other crops, is typified by South Carolina. Still, cotton is the crop of third highest value, following soybeans and tobacco. Corn places fourth in value (1974). Mineral production, based on stone and clay, is less valuable than that of any other Southern state.

South Carolina's rate of population increase (mainly a natural increase) has been rapid during the 1970's—9.9 percent between April 1, 1970, and July 1, 1976. Manufacturing employment has increased relative to most states, amounting to 1.41 percent of the national total in the 1958 Census of Manufactures and 1.82 percent of the total in 1972.

Textiles and apparel are by far the leading industrial fields. While North Carolina is well in the lead in this field of manufacturing, South Carolina was ahead of the substantial Georgia textile industry in 1972. A great deal of employment is provided by the textile industry because it is so labor intensive. In South Carolina in 1972, after deduction by the author of the estimated contribution of professional persons, labor accounted for 44 percent of the value added by manufacturing in the textile industry. This is somewhat higher than in the other leading textile producing states.

Greenville is the largest of the South Carolina textile cities. It produces a wide variety of synthetic, cotton, and woolen textile fabrics.[11] Clothing manufacturing has grown markedly in the city. As is often the case near an urban area (even around New York City) the nearby farms tend to specialize in food production for the city market.

[11] Detailed industry information for South Carolina is from Bogue and Beale, pp. 996-1005.

Other cities in Northwestern South Carolina, such as Spartanburg, Anderson, and Greenwood, as well as many small towns in the vicinity employ over 50,000 textile mill workers.

To the East, in the North Central part of the state, economic development is less advanced, but the concentration on textiles still exists. Rock Hill is a principal manufacturing city. On a smaller scale, textile production takes place also in Central South Carolina.

Charleston, founded in 1680, has long been an important seaport. Manufacturing in the city and surrounding area is based heavily on processing materials that enter into trade at the port such as fertilizer, asbestos, paper products, cigars, oil products, and apparel.

Only North Carolina has a lower percentage of non-farm workers in unions. As of 1972, 9 percent of such labor was organized in South Carolina, compared with 7.5 percent in North Carolina and a national average of 27.2 percent.

South Dakota

Corn is the most valuable crop in South Dakota, with wheat, hay, and oats next in value. Altogether the crops in 1974 were valued at about $1.1 billion. Mineral output is low, with gold the most valuable in 1973.

South Dakota is divided roughly into two parts, East and West, by the Missouri River. The Western area is sparsely populated ranch country with a population of only about 150,000. (The entire State added only 5 percent to its population in the first six years of the present decade.)

Geologically the Western area is very interesting, in some places containing the South Dakota Badlands where countless peaks, pinnacles, spires, and other formations are of tourist interest. The Black Hills have gold, uranium, and other mineral products. Mount Rushmore attracts thousands of tourists each year.

Rapid City is the major city of Western South Dakota, providing shopping, wholesale, supply, and marketing activity for the region.

The most productive farming area is the extreme Southeast of South Dakota. The adequate rainfall and longer growing season are favorable for corn, and feed grain yields are good. This is also the most urbanized area of the State, with the manufacturing activities, such as meat packing and cereals, based largely on surrounding agriculture. Sioux Falls, the only large city in the area, is the commercial center for a broad region.

Pierre, the capital city, is in the center of the State. To the Northeast, Aberdeen and Huron dominate a relatively urban section. Growth of the cities has offset the decline in farm population. Manufacturing consists largely of food products but the cities are important in providing retail and wholesale marketing for large rural areas.

Tennessee

Eastern Tennessee's economic development has been greatly aided by federal government investment in the Tennessee Valley Authority and Oak Ridge. Knoxville is the headquarters of TVA and also the location of the University of Tennessee. In and around Knoxville clothing, especially men's clothing, is manufactured on a substantial scale, as are products for industry, plastic articles, furniture, and other goods. Not far to the South, the twin cities of Maryville and Alcoa are the site of one of the largest aluminum sheet rolling mills.

Chattanooga, to the Southwest near the Georgia border, has well-diversified industry. Textile mills are the largest employers. Both metal and wood products of numerous sorts are turned out. Foods, glassware, paper, and farm machinery are other products.

Nashville in central Tennessee is the only city of size in that area. In addition to being a university town, Nashville has an exceptionally varied economy including durable goods such as stoves, electrical appliances, furniture and auto glass. Non-durables include nylon, cellophane, food products, shoes, clothing and publications.

The other large city is Memphis, on the East bank of the Mississippi River. Memphis is the commercial capital for much of the lower Mississippi valley. The city is a large cotton market, hardwood lumber market, and wholesale distribution center. Banking is consequently a flourishing activity. Manufacturing is well-diversified, including wood products, cottonseed oil, paper products, textiles, farm machinery, fertilizer, and livestock feeds.

According to the 1972 Census of Manufactures, for Tennessee as a whole, chemicals and allied products, electrical equipment, and food products lead in value added by manufacture. Other principal growth industries are leather, textiles, paper, and apparel.[12]

Soybeans and corn have taken first and second place among Tennessee's agricultural crops with the older products, tobacco and cotton following in value (1974).

Population grew at a moderate 7.3 percent between April 1, 1970, and July 1, 1976. The proportion of non-farm workers belonging to unions is rather high for a Southern Right-to-Work state (18.4 percent in 1972) in part because of the substantial importance of aluminum production and of mining.

---

[12] M. R. Colberg, *Human Capital in Southern Development: 1939–1963* (Chapel Hill: University of North Carolina Press, 1965), p. 84.

Texas

The Texas economy is difficult to describe briefly because of its size and diversity. Population increased by 1,238,000 in the six years ending July 1, 1976. The State leads by far in mineral output with petroleum, natural gas, and other products valued at almost $8.5 billion in 1973. Only Iowa among Right-to-Work states exceeds Texas in agricultural output. Cotton, sorghum, rice, and wheat led in value in 1974. In value of shipments of manufactured goods Texas also leads the Right-to-Work states (Table 3.7).

Houston seems to epitomize the wealth and growth of the Texas economy. It is the leading manufacturing center in the South. Its skyline is characterized by tall new buildings with large expanses of glass that suggest no fear of an energy crisis.

Dallas, in North Central Texas, is a financial and insurance center. Employment of women is large because of the number of white collar jobs. Aircraft and missile production have become large operations since the outbreak of World War II. Automobile assembly and electronic equipment also supplement the older industrial base of apparel, oilfield equipment, and cotton gin machinery.

Fort Worth, also in North Central Texas, is almost contiguous with Dallas if outlying districts are considered. This has made possible the recent construction of a giant airfield for joint use. Fort Worth has long been a leading cattle and sheep market. In part, the economy is similar to that of Dallas, with aircraft and automotive industries. Some of the closest oil fields have been depleted but the industry still is important to the city.

Western Texas is arid and lightly inhabited. Very large ranches prevail but agriculture is possible only where irrigation water is available. Surprisingly lush growth occurs in places along the Rio Grande and Pecos Rivers. Oilfields in the area have partially replaced those to the East. A large part of the population is of Spanish descent and for the most part poor.

In the extreme South of Texas the land is also arid. The extremely large King ranch and the town of Kingville are features. Oil and natural gas are produced in the region. Corpus Christi on the Gulf is a booming city, although it was a small town as late as 1920. Oil refineries, shipping, naval activities, and manufacturing based on oil and gas predominate.

A little to the North, San Antonio, with its famous Alamo has become a large city. Its economy is based more on trade and government employment, both military and civilian, than on manufacturing.

Austin, the capital of Texas, is also the location of the University of Texas. As often occurs in such a city, manufacturing is not of primary importance. Agriculture in the area is rather typical of Central Texas, with cotton, cattle, and dairy operations.

Utah

North Central Utah has the State's main concentration of urban activity, with Salt Lake City, Ogden, Provo, and Logan all located there. This general region is also best for agriculture, with the aid of irrigation. Hay, wheat, barley, and sugarbeets led in 1974 value among the crops, but poultry farming, including turkeys, is a large specialty.

Salt Lake City is the dominant political, educational, and religious center of the State. A large copper mining operation takes place within the metropolitan area, contributing to this metal's lead in the State over petroleum, coal, and gold as the principal minerals. Mineral output was valued at about two-thirds of a billion dollars in 1973.

Ogden, 37 miles North of Salt Lake City, has a diversified economy based in large part on easily available timber, coal, and metallic ores. Manufacturing activities include textiles and apparel, meat packing, iron and steel products, sugar refining and canning of foods.

South of Salt Lake City, Provo has steel mills, smelters, canneries, and sugar refineries.

Southern Utah is quite different, being arid and without significant urban concentrations. A large percentage of the land has no present economic use except, where accessible to tourists, for its high scenic value. Mining operations are scattered throughout the vast area. Iron County produces iron ore for Western steel mills. Bituminous coal underlies large areas, with Carbon and Emery Counties being important producers. Since oil bearing shale is also common, Utah has much potential for development in an energy-short economy.

Unionization of labor is rather low at 14.9 percent of the non-agricultural labor force, down from 20.9 percent in 1970. Population grew at a rapid 15.9 percent rate from April 1, 1970, to July 1, 1976. Presumably most of the new inhabitants did not become union members.

Virginia

Northern Virginia just South of Washington, D.C., like nearby Maryland, is a metropolitan appendage of the capital city. The Pentagon and other military installations are especially important to employment in the Northern Virginia economy. Arlington County is among the richest counties in the nation in median family income.

A hundred miles to the South, Richmond, the capital, is an industrial, commercial, and governmental center. Tobacco is Virginia's principal agricultural crop and Richmond is a tobacco products center.

Most of the leading cigarette companies have plants in the city. Richmond is also a baking center and a producer of textiles, apparel, and fabricated steel.

To the East, where Chesapeake Bay meets the Atlantic Ocean, Norfolk and Portsmouth form a substantial urbanized area. The armed forces provide a large part of the employment due to the Naval base at Norfolk and the Naval shipyard at Portsmouth. Truck crops are raised in the vicinity, partly for shipment to Northern markets.

Across the State to the West, Roanoke is a railroad center, including manufacture and repair of freight cars. Within the city and nearby are several textile mills and apparel plants as well as furniture factories. Several hundred commercial farms in the area sell milk, livestock, poultry, apples, and peaches. Since Roanoke is the only city of substantial size in Western Virginia, it serves as a trading and commercial center for the area.

Southeast of Roanoke, near the North Carolina border, is Danville with its huge Dan River Mills textile complex. Danville is also a large tobacco market as tobacco has long been the backbone of the adjacent farm economy.

Southwest Virginia is the coal fields area. While not extensive in size it is highly productive, making coal Virginia's most valuable mineral product. Livestock and dairy farms predominate as the land is ill-suited to tillage.

Virginia's leading crops, after tobacco, are corn, hay, and soybeans. Apples and peaches, turkeys and broilers, wheat and fisheries are of importance to various sections. Chemicals and allied products, food products, and electrical equipment lead in value added by manufacture in the two-digit Census of Manufactures industry groupings.

Population increased at a fairly rapid rate (8.2 percent) from April 1, 1970, to July 1, 1976. Non-farm workers were organized to the extent of 15.5 percent in 1972, about average for the Right-to-Work states and well below the nation's average.

Wyoming

Wyoming is growing rapidly in population, 17.4 percent between April 1, 1970, and July 1, 1976. Unionization of non-agricultural workers is fairly high at 18.2 percent and has not changed much in this respect in the last decade.

Northwestern Wyoming is dominated by two very popular national parks, Yellowstone (partly in Wyoming) and Grand Teton just to the South.

East of the center of the State, Casper is the second largest city. Its location and good transportation facilities make it a leading wholesale trade center. There is also petroleum refining based on nearby oil wells. Petroleum, sodium compounds, uranium, and natural gas led an almost $1 billion dollar mineral production industry in the State in 1973. The important energy-related extraction and processing potential should continue to bring economic growth to Wyoming.

Agriculture is followed on irrigated lands, while grazing is possible on some of the nonirrigated lands. Hay, sugarbeets, wheat, and barley led the crops in 1973 value. Wyoming's farm output was valued at less than a quarter billion dollars, however, ahead of only Utah and Nevada among Right-to-Work states.

Cheyenne, the largest city and the State capital, resembles Denver on a smaller scale in that it is located just east of the Rockies and serves a large number of functions as the largest city. In addition to being a railroad center, Cheyenne plants make aircraft instruments and service a large Air Force base. The employment of government and commercial workers is extensive.

SUMMER 1977

Policy Review 1

The International Standard Serial Number for *Policy Review* is ISSN: 0146-5945.

FALL 1977 **Policy Review** 2

The International Standard Serial Number for *Policy Review* is ISSN: 0146-5945.